THE GOLDEN SONG BOOK

Selected and arranged by
KATHARINE TYLER WESSELLS

Illustrated by KATHY ALLERT

Guitar chords by Christopher Clarke

A GOLDEN PRESS • NEW YORK

Western Publishing Company, Inc., Racine, Wisconsin 53404

Dedicated to Kathleen

Acknowledgment

The compiler and the publishers acknowledge
with gratitude the invaluable assistance of
Kurt Stone in the preparation of this book.

CONTENTS

Suggestions for singing games have been included for some songs. These are indicated by asterisks.

THE FARMER IN THE DELL

GAME: Children form a ring with one child as "farmer" in the middle. They join hands and sing while marching around the farmer. The "farmer" chooses a "wife," etc. Finally the "cheese" is clapped out and must begin again as farmer.

Old singing game · Harmonized by Katharine Tyler Wessells · Words and tune traditional

The farm-er in the dell, The farm-er in the dell, Heigh-o, the der-ry-o, The farm-er in the dell.

The dog takes a cat,
The dog takes a cat,
Heigh-o, the derry-o,
The dog takes a cat.

The cat takes a rat,
The cat takes a rat,
Heigh-o, the derry-o,
The cat takes a rat.

The rat takes a cheese,
The rat takes a cheese,
Heigh-o, the derry-o,
The rat takes a cheese.

The cheese stands alone!
The cheese stands alone!
Heigh-o, the derry-o,
The cheese stands alone!

The farmer takes a wife,
The farmer takes a wife,
Heigh-ho, the derry-o,
The farmer takes a wife.

The wife takes a child,
The wife takes a child,
Heigh-o, the derry-o,
The wife takes a child.

The child takes a nurse,
The child takes a nurse,
Heigh-o, the derry-o,
The child takes a nurse.

The nurse takes a dog,
The nurse takes a dog,
Heigh-o, the derry-o,
The nurse takes a dog.

ROW, ROW, ROW YOUR BOAT

Old round

Harmonized by Katharine Tyler Wessells

Words and tune traditional

Row, row, row your boat, Gent - ly down the stream,

Mer - ri - ly, mer - ri - ly, mer - ri - ly, mer - ri - ly, Life is but a dream.

HICKORY, DICKORY, DOCK

Words from Mother Goose

Harmonized by Katharine Tyler Wessells

Tune traditional

Hick - o - ry, dick - o - ry, dock! The mouse ran up the clock; The

clock struck one, The mouse ran down, Hick - o - ry, dick - o - ry, dock!

9

OLD MACDONALD HAD A FARM

Words and tune traditional

Harmonized by Katharine Tyler Wessells

Old Mac-Don-ald had a farm, Ee - igh, ee - igh, oh! And

on this farm he had some chicks, Ee - igh, ee - igh, oh! With a

chick, chick here and a chick, chick there; Here a chick, there a chick,

Every-where a chick, chick. Old Mac-Don-ald had a farm, Ee-igh, ee-igh, oh!

Old MacDonald had a farm, Ee-igh, ee-igh, oh!
And on this farm he had some ducks, Ee-igh, ee-igh, oh!
With a quack, quack here, and a quack, quack there;
Here a quack, there a quack, everywhere a quack, quack,
With a chick, chick here, and a chick, chick there,
Here a chick, there a chick, everywhere a chick, chick.
Old MacDonald had a farm, Ee-igh, ee-igh, oh!

Old MacDonald had a farm, Ee-igh, ee-igh, oh!
And on this farm he had some turkeys, Ee-igh, ee-igh, oh!
With a gobble, gobble here, and a gobble, gobble there;
Here a gobble, there a gobble, everywhere a gobble, gobble,
With a quack, quack here, and a quack, quack there;
Here a quack, there a quack, everywhere a quack, quack,
With a chick, chick here, and a chick, chick there;
Here a chick, there a chick, everywhere a chick, chick.
Old MacDonald had a farm, Ee-igh, ee-igh, oh!

Old MacDonald had a farm, Ee-igh, ee-igh, oh!
And on this farm he had some pigs, Ee-igh, ee-igh, oh!
With an oink, oink here, and an oink, oink there;
Here an oink, there an oink, everywhere an oink, oink,
With a gobble, gobble here, and a gobble, gobble there;
Here a gobble, there a gobble, everywhere a gobble, gobble,
With a quack, quack here, and a quack, quack there;
Here a quack, there a quack, everywhere a quack, quack,
With a chick, chick here, and a chick, chick there;
Here a chick, there a chick, everywhere a chick, chick.
Old MacDonald had a farm, Ee-igh, ee-igh, oh!

Old MacDonald had a farm, Ee-igh, ee-igh, oh!
And on this farm he had some cows, Ee-igh, ee-igh, oh!
With a moo, moo here, etc.

Old MacDonald had a farm, Ee-igh, ee-igh, oh!
And on this farm he had some donkeys, Ee-igh, ee-igh, oh!
With a hee, haw here, etc.

11

MARY HAD A LITTLE LAMB

Words and tune traditional

Harmonized by Katharine Tyler Wessells

Ma - ry had a lit - tle lamb, lit - tle lamb, lit - tle lamb,

Ma - ry had a lit - tle lamb, Its fleece was white as snow.

And everywhere that Mary went,
Mary went, Mary went,
Everywhere that Mary went,
The lamb was sure to go.

It followed her to school one day,
School one day, school one day,
Followed her to school one day,
Which was against the rule.

It made the children laugh and play,
Laugh and play, laugh and play,
Made the children laugh and play,
To see a lamb at school.

12

ROUND THE MULBERRY BUSH

GAME: Suit the actions to the words.

Harmonized by Katharine Tyler Wessells

Singing game

Words and tune traditional

Here we go round the mul-ber-ry bush, The mul-ber-ry bush, the mul-ber-ry bush;

Here we go round the mul-ber-ry bush, So ear-ly in ___ the morn-ing.

This is the way we wash our clothes,
We wash our clothes, we wash our clothes;
This is the way we wash our clothes,
So early Monday morning.

This is the way we iron our clothes,
We iron our clothes, we iron our clothes;
This is the way we iron our clothes,
So early Tuesday morning.

This is the way we scrub the floor,
We scrub the floor, we scrub the floor;
This is the way we scrub the floor,
So early Wednesday morning.

This is the way we mend our clothes,
We mend our clothes, we mend our clothes;
This is the way we mend our clothes,
So early Thursday morning.

This is the way we sweep the house,
We sweep the house, we sweep the house;
This is the way we sweep the house,
So early Friday morning.

This is the way we bake our bread,
We bake our bread, we bake our bread;
This is the way we bake our bread,
So early Saturday morning.

This is the way we go to church,
We go to church, we go to church;
This is the way we go to church,
So early Sunday morning.

A TISKET, A TASKET

GAME: This is a "drop-the-handkerchief" game. Children, holding each other's hands, stand in a circle. The child who is "it," carrying the handkerchief, runs around the outside, while they all sing. He drops the handkerchief when he comes to the person of his choice, and then continues running around the circle. The other child runs in the opposite direction, and each tries to reach the vacant place first. The one who is last takes the handkerchief for the next round.

Old singing game   Harmonized by Katharine Tyler Wessells   Words and tune traditional

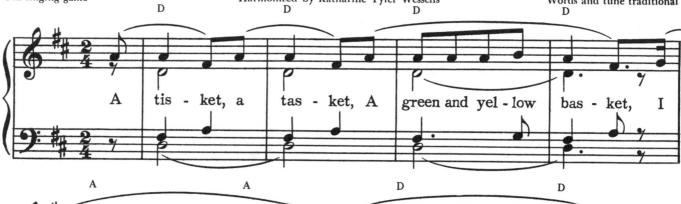

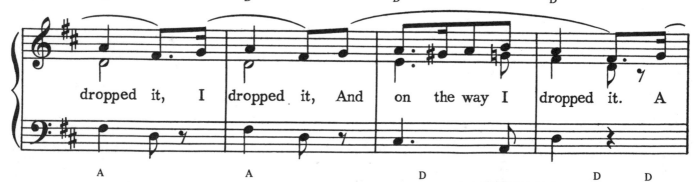

FRÈRE JACQUES

Old French round Harmonized by Katharine Tyler Wessells Words, tune, and translation traditional

Frè-re Jacques, Frè-re Jacques, Dor-mez vous? Dor-mez vous? Son-nez les ma-
Are you sleeping? Are you sleeping, Brother John, Broth-er John? Morning bells are

ti - nes, Son-nez les ma - ti - nes: Din, Din, Don, Din, Din, Don.
ring-ing, Morning bells are ring-ing: Ding, Ding, Dong, Ding, Ding, Dong.

15

SING A SONG OF SIXPENCE

Words from Mother Goose Harmonized by Katharine Tyler Wessells Melody by J. W. Elliott

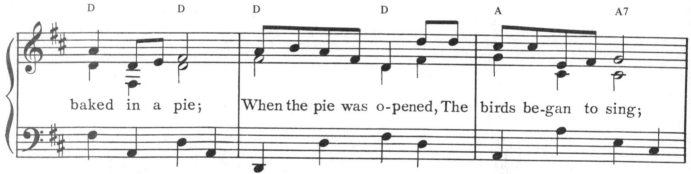

Sing a song of six-pence, A pock-et full of rye, Four and twen-ty black-birds

baked in a pie; When the pie was o-pened, The birds be-gan to sing;

Was-n't that a dain-ty dish to set be-fore a king? The

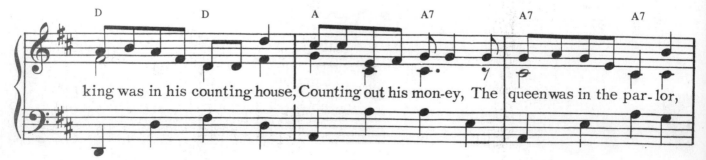

king was in his counting house, Counting out his mon-ey, The queen was in the par-lor,

Eat - ing bread and hon - ey, The maid was in the gar - den,

Hang-ing out the clothes, There came a lit - tle black-bird and pecked off her nose.

LITTLE BOY BLUE

Words from Mother Goose Harmonized by Katharine Tyler Wessells Tune traditional

Lit - tle Boy Blue, come blow your horn, The sheep's in the meadow the cow's in the corn.

Where is the boy who looks af - ter the sheep? He's un - der the hay-stack fast a - sleep.

17

BAA, BAA, BLACK SHEEP

Words from Mother Goose

Harmonized by Katharine Tyler Wessells

Tune traditional

"Baa, baa, black sheep, have you an-y wool?" "Yes sir, yes sir, three bags full,

One for my mas-ter and one for my dame, And one for the lit-tle boy that lives in the lane."

JACK AND JILL

Words from Mother Goose

Harmonized by Katharine Tyler Wessells

Melody by J. W. Elliott

Jack and Jill went up the hill, To fetch a pail of wa - ter.

Jack fell down and broke his crown, And Jill came tum-bling af - ter.

Then up Jack got, and home did trot,
As fast as he could caper.
He went to bed and plastered his head
With vinegar and brown paper.

Jill came in and she did grin,
To see his paper plaster.
Mother, vexed, did whip her next,
For causing Jack's disaster.

ROUND THE VILLAGE

GAME: Children stand in a circle and pretend they are houses in a village. One child is "it" and runs round and round the village during the first verse. At the second verse the children join hands and raise their arms high to make windows, while the child runs in and out. During the third verse, the child looks around the circle, pauses, and then chooses a partner. At the fourth verse ("Follow me to London") the first child leads his partner around the circle; but they return at the end of the verse to the center of the circle, where they shake hands, bow, and part (fifth verse). The first child then takes his place in the circle and the second is "it."

Old singing game   Harmonized by Katharine Tyler Wessells   Words and tune traditional

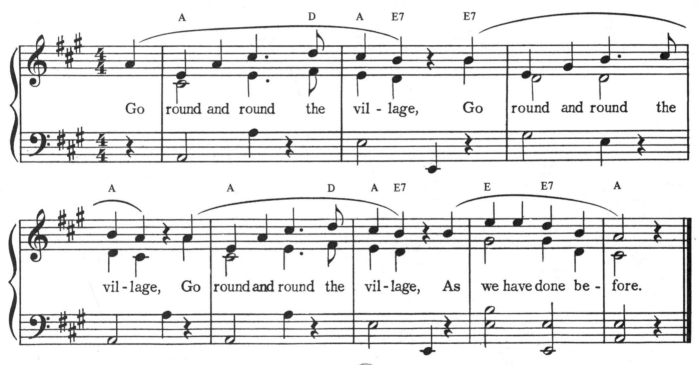

Go round and round the vil - lage, Go round and round the vil - lage, Go round and round the vil - lage, As we have done be - fore.

Go in and out the windows,
Go in and out the windows,
Go in and out the windows,
As we have done before.

Now stand and face your partner,
Now stand and face your partner,
Now stand and face your partner,
And bow before you go.

Now follow me to London,
Now follow me to London,
Now follow me to London,
As we have done before.

Now shake his hand and leave him,
Now shake his hand and leave him,
Now shake his hand and leave him,
And bow before you go.

19

OATS, PEAS, BEANS, AND BARLEY GROW

GAME: Children, singing, circle around a child in the middle (the farmer), suiting gestures to words. At the third verse the farmer chooses a partner, and at the fourth verse they both kneel and salute.

Old singing game Harmonized by Katharine Tyler Wessells Tune traditional (French)

Oats, peas, beans, and bar - ley grows, Oats, peas, beans, and bar - ley grows, Nor you nor I nor an - y - one knows How oats, peas, beans, and bar - ley grows.

Thus the farmer sows his seed,
Stands erect and takes his ease,
He stamps his foot and claps his hands,
And turns around to view his lands.

Waiting for a partner,
Waiting for a partner,
Open the ring and take her in,
While we all gaily dance and sing.

SHE'LL BE COMIN' 'ROUND THE MOUNTAIN

Old American chanty

Harmonized by Katharine Tyler Wessells

Words and music traditional

She'll be com-in' round the moun-tain when she comes, _____ when she

comes She'll be com-in' round the moun-tain when she comes, _____ when she

comes She'll be com-in' round the moun-tain, She'll be com-in' round the

moun-tain, She'll be com-in' round the moun-tain when she comes! _____

when she comes!

She'll be drivin' six white horses when she comes, etc.

We will all be out to meet her when she comes, etc.

21

A FROG HE WOULD A-WOOING GO

Words and tune from Ednah P. C. Hayes

Harmonized by Katharine Tyler Wessells

A frog, he would a-woo-ing go, Hm - m, hm - m, Frog he would a-woo-ing go, And he dressed himself from top to toe, Hm - m, hm - m.

"Uncle Rat, is Miss Mouse within?
Hm-m, hm-m-m,
Uncle Rat, is Miss Mouse within?"
"Yes, in the parlor, learning to spin,
Hm-m, hm-m-m."

"Oh, Miss Mouse, will you marry me?
Hm-m, hm-m-m,
Oh, Miss Mouse, will you marry me?"
"Yes, if Uncle Rat will agree,
Hm-m, hm-m-m."

"Uncle Rat has gone to town.
Hm-m, hm-m-m,
Uncle Rat has gone to town,
To buy Miss Mouse a wedding gown,
Hm-m, hm-m-m."

"Where shall the wedding supper be?
Hm-m, hm-m-m,
Where shall the wedding supper be?"
"Way down yonder in the hollow tree,
Hm-m, hm-m-m."

First came in was the old tom-cat,
Hm-m, hm-m-m,
First came in was the old tom-cat,
And he danced a jig with Mistress Rat,
Hm-m, hm-m-m.

Next came in was the bumble-bee,
Hm-m, hm-m-m,
Next came in was the bumble-bee,
And he danced a jig with old Miss Flea,
Hm-m, hm-m-m.

"And what do you think they had for supper?
Hm-m, hm-m-m,
And what do you think they had for supper?"
"Black-eyed peas, corn pone, and butter,
Hm-m, hm-m-m."

"And what do you think they had to drink?
Hm-m, hm-m-m,
And what do you think they had to drink?"
"Persimmon beer and a bottle of ink,
Hm-m, hm-m-m."

And after supper the old tom-cat,
Hm-m, hm-m-m,
And after supper the old tom-cat,
He ate up the frog, the mouse, and the rat,
Hm-m, hm-m-m.

Saddle and bridle on the shelf,
Hm-m, hm-m-m,
Saddle and bridle on the shelf,
If you want any more you can sing it yourself,
Hm-m, hm-m-m.

HEY DIDDLE DIDDLE

Words from Mother Goose Harmonized by Katharine Tyler Wessells Tune traditional

Hey, did-dle, did-dle, the cat and the fid-dle, The cow jumped o-ver the moon;— The lit-tle dog laughed to see such sport, And the dish ran a-way with the spoon, spoon, spoon, The dish ran a-way with the spoon.

24

POP! GOES THE WEASEL

Words and tune traditional

Harmonized by Katharine Tyler Wessells

All a-round the cob-bler's bench, The mon-key chased the wea-sel, The

mon-key thought 'twas all in fun, Pop! goes the wea-sel. A

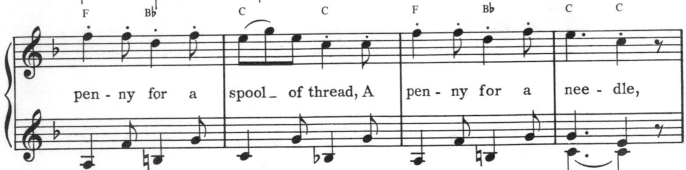

pen-ny for a spool of thread, A pen-ny for a nee-dle,

That's the way the mon-ey goes, Pop! goes the wea-sel.

25

DID YOU EVER SEE A LASSIE?

GAME: Form a single circle, hands joined, with one child in center. Measures 1-8: Skip around to the left during the first two lines of song. As words "do this way and that" are sung, the child in the center imitates some activity. Measures 9-16: All drop hands, face center of circle, and imitate leader.

Old singing game

Harmonized by Katharine Tyler Wessells

Words and tune traditional

Did you ev - er see a las - sie, a / lad - die, a las - sie, a / lad - die, a las - sie? / lad - die? Did you

ev - er see a las - sie / lad - die go this way and that? Go

this way and that way and this way and that way? Did you

ev - er see a las - sie / lad - die go this way and that?

26

RIDE A COCK-HORSE

Words from Mother Goose   Harmonized by Katharine Tyler Wessells   Melody by J. W. Elliott

Ride a cock-horse, to Ban-bur-y Cross, To see a fine la-dy up-on a white horse; Rings on her fin-gers, and bells on her toes, She shall have mu-sic wher-ev-er she goes.

YANKEE DOODLE

Words and tune traditional

Harmonized by Katharine Tyler Wessells

Yan-kee Doo-dle went to town up - on a lit - tle po - ny, He

stuck a feath-er in his cap and called it mac-a - ro - ni.

Yan - kee Doo-dle, Doo-dle Doo, Yan - kee Doo-dle Dan - dy,

All the las-sies are so smart and sweet as sug-ar can-dy.

Fath'r and I went down to camp,
Along with Captain Goodin,
And there we saw the men and boys,
As thick as hasty puddin'.

Yankee Doodle keep it up,
Yankee Doodle dandy,
Mind the music and the step,
and with the girls be handy.

SCOTLAND'S BURNING

Harmonized by Katharine Tyler Wessells

Old round

Words and tune traditional

Scot-land's burn-ing, Scot-land's burn-ing, Look out! Look out!

Fire! Fire! Fire! Fire! Pour on wa-ter, Pour on wa-ter.

29

OH, DEAR! WHAT CAN THE MATTER BE?

Words and tune traditional

Harmonized by Katharine Tyler Wessells

Oh, dear! What can the mat-ter be? Dear, dear! What can the mat-ter be?

Oh, dear! What can the mat-ter be? John-ny's so long at the fair. __ He

promised he'd buy me a fairing should please me, And then for a kiss, Oh, he vowed he would tease me, He

promised he'd buy me a bunch of blue ribbons, To tie up my bonnie brown hair. __

Oh, dear! What can the mat-ter be? Dear, dear! What can the mat-ter be?

Oh, dear! What can the mat-ter be? John-ny's so long at the fair.

LONDON BRIDGE

GAME: Two players represent the bridge by joining hands and raising them to form an arch. The rest of the children, in single line or couples, pass under the bridge. When the words "My fair lady" are sung, the two keepers of the bridge let their arms fall, catching whichever child happens to be passing under at the time. He then is asked the question, "Do you choose gold or silver?" The keepers have privately agreed which of these words each will represent. The prisoner then stands behind the child representing his choice. When all have been caught, the game ends with a tug of war between the two sides.

Singing game

Harmonized by Katharine Tyler Wessells

Words and tune traditional

Lon - don Bridge is fall - ing down, Fall - ing down, fall - ing down,

Lon - don Bridge is fall - ing down, My fair la - dy!

Build it up with iron bars, etc.

Iron bars will bend and break, etc.

Build it up with pins and needles, etc.

Pins and needles rust and bend, etc.

Build it up with penny loaves, etc.

Penny loaves will tumble down, etc.

Build it up with gold and silver, etc.

Gold and silver I've not got, etc.

Here's a prisoner I have got, etc.

What's the prisoner done to you, etc.

Stole my watch and broke my chain, etc.

What'll you take to set him free, etc.

One hundred pounds will set him free, etc.

One hundred pounds we have not got, etc.

Then off to prison he must go, etc.

32

LOOBY-LOO

GAME: Form a single circle, hands joined. Skip to left until words "Saturday night" are sung. All put right hands in toward the center of the circle, then stretch right hands away from the center of the circle. All shake right hands hard and turn in place. Repeat for following verses, suiting action to words.

Old singing game

Words and tune traditional

Here we dance Loo-by - loo, Here we dance Loo-by - light,

Here we dance Loo-by - loo, All on a Sat-ur - day night. ___ I

put my right hand in, ___ I put my right hand out, ___ I

give my right hand a shake, shake, shake, And turn my-self a - bout.

I put my left hand in, etc.   I put my right foot in, etc.   I put my left foot in, etc.

I put my little head in, etc.   I put my whole self in, etc.

33

HUMPTY DUMPTY

Words from Mother Goose

Tune and arrangement by J. W. Elliott

Hump - ty Dump - ty sat on a wall, Hump - ty Dump - ty

had a great fall. All the King's hors - es and all the King's men

Could-n't put Hump - ty Dump - ty to - geth - er a - gain.

34

BILLY BOY

Words and tune traditional

Harmonized by Katharine Tyler Wessells

Oh,— where have you been, Bil-ly Boy, Bil-ly Boy, Oh,— where have you been, charming Bil-ly?— I have been to seek a wife, She's the joy— of my life, She's a young thing and can-not leave her moth-er.—

Did she bid you to come in, Billy Boy, Billy Boy?
Did she bid you to come in, charming Billy?
    She's a young thing and cannot leave her mother.

Yes, she bade me to come in,
There's a dimple in her chin,

Did she set for you a chair, Billy Boy, Billy Boy?
Did she set for you a chair, charming Billy?
    She's a young thing and cannot leave her mother.

Yes, she set for me a chair,
She has ringlets in her hair,

Can she make a cherry pie, Billy Boy, Billy Boy?
Can she make a cherry pie, charming Billy?
    She's a young thing and cannot leave her mother.

She can make a cherry pie,
Quick's a cat can wink her eye,

THE MUFFIN MAN

GAME: Form one large circle with hands joined, skipping to the left. A child stands in the center and chooses a partner from the big circle by skipping toward the chosen one and offering both hands on the words, "Oh, yes we've seen the Muffin Man." The two occupying the center now join both hands and sing "Two have seen the Muffin Man" to the end of this verse. At the beginning of the next verse, these two choose partners from the ring, and the four join hands, singing, "Four have seen the Muffin Man." This is repeated until all are chosen and the big circle sings, "All have seen the Muffin Man." The two circles move in contrary directions.

Old singing game   Harmonized by Katharine Tyler Wessells   Words and tune traditional

Oh, do you know the Muf-fin Man, The Muf-fin Man, the Muf-fin Man, Oh, do you know the Muf-fin Man, That lives in Dru-ry Lane? Oh!

Oh, yes we've seen the Muffin Man,
The Muffin Man, the Muffin Man;
Oh, yes we've seen the Muffin Man,
That lives in Drury Lane! Oh!

36

I HAD A LITTLE NUT TREE

Words from Mother Goose Harmonized by Katharine Tyler Wessells Tune traditional

I had a lit-tle nut tree; noth-ing would it bear, But a sil-ver nut-meg and a gold-en pear. The King of Spain's daugh-ter came to vis-it me, And all — for the sake of my lit-tle nut tree.

JINGLE BELLS

Words traditional   Arranged by Katharine Tyler Wessells   Tune by J. Pierpont

Dashing through the snow,   in a one-horse o - pen sleigh,   And o'er the fields we go,   Laughing all the way.   The bells on bob-tail ring, Mak-ing spir-its bright. What fun it is to ride and sing A sleighing song to-night.

THREE BLIND MICE

Words from Mother Goose

Harmonized by Katharine Tyler Wessells

Tune traditional

Three blind mice, — Three blind mice, — See how they run! — See how they run! — They all ran af-ter the farm-er's wife, Who cut off their tails with a carv-ing knife. Did you ev-er see such a sight in your life As three blind mice?

ROCKABYE, BABY

Words and tune traditional

Harmonized by Katharine Tyler Wessells

Rock - a - bye, ba - by, on the tree - top.

When the wind blows, the cra-dle will rock; When the bough breaks, the

cra-dle will fall, And down will come ba - by, cra-dle and all.

POLLY PUT THE KETTLE ON

Words from Mother Goose Harmonized by Katharine Tyler Wessells Tune traditional (English)

Pol-ly put the ket-tle on, Pol-ly put the ket-tle on, Pol-ly put the ket-tle on, We'll all have tea! Su-key, take it off a-gain, Su-key, take it off a-gain, Su-key, take it off a-gain, They've all gone a-way.

AU CLAIR DE LA LUNE

French words traditional   Translated and harmonized by Katharine Tyler Wessells   Melody attributed to Lully (1633-1687)

Au clair de la lune, Mon a - mi, Pier - rot,
In the eve-ning moon-light, My good friend, Pier-rot,

Prêt-e moi ta plu - me, Pour é - crire un mot.
Lend to me your quill-pen, Just to write a note.

Ma chan-delle est mor - te, Je n'ai plus de feu;
My can-dle is burnt out, And my fire's out too;

Ou - vre moi ta por - te Pour l'a-mour de Dieu.
Your front door please o - pen, Please, I beg of you.

43

TWINKLE, TWINKLE, LITTLE STAR

Words traditional

Harmonized by Katharine Tyler Wessells

Old French air

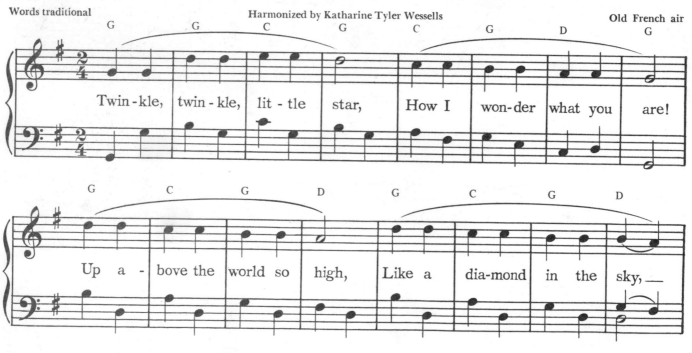

Twin-kle, twin-kle, lit-tle star, How I won-der what you are!

Up a - bove the world so high, Like a dia-mond in the sky, ___

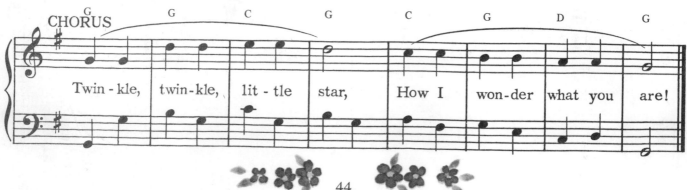

CHORUS

Twin-kle, twin-kle, lit-tle star, How I won-der what you are!

CRADLE SONG

Words traditional   Arranged by Katharine Tyler Wessells   Music by Johannes Brahms

Lul-la - by and good-night, With ros - es be-

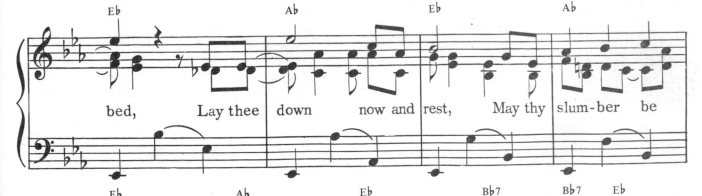

dight, __ With lil - ies be - decked Is __ ba - by's wee

bed, Lay thee down now and rest, May thy slum-ber be

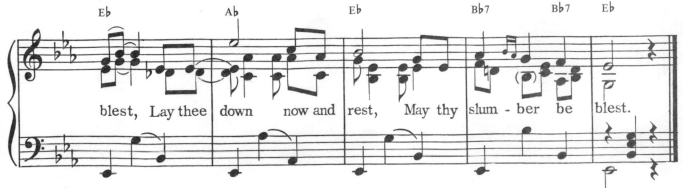

blest, Lay thee down now and rest, May thy slum - ber be blest.